Bring Him Home

from *Les Misérables*

arranged for harp by Sylvia Woods

Music by Claude-Michel Schönberg
Lyrics by Alain Boublil, Jean-Marc Natel and Herbert Kretzmer

Bring Him Home
from *Les Misérables*

Music by Claude-Michel Schönberg
Lyrics by Herbert Kretzmer and Alain Boublil
Harp arrangement by Sylvia Woods

Please note that both hands begin in the treble clef.

Sharping lever changes are indicated with diamond notes and also with octave wording.
Pedal changes are written below the bass staff.

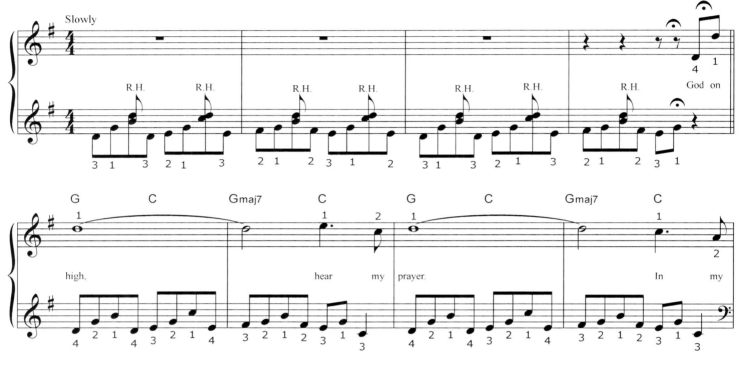

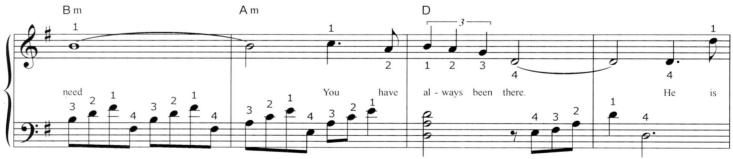

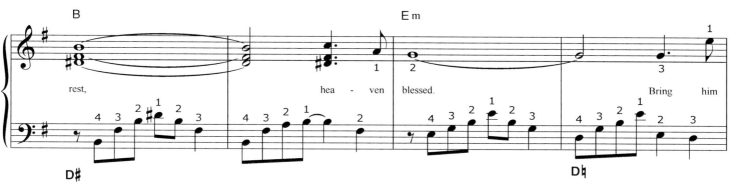

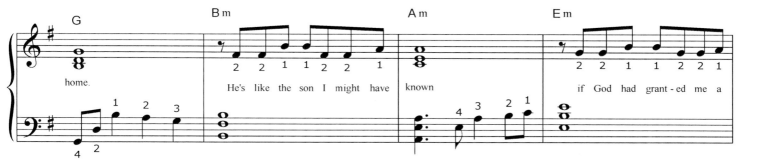

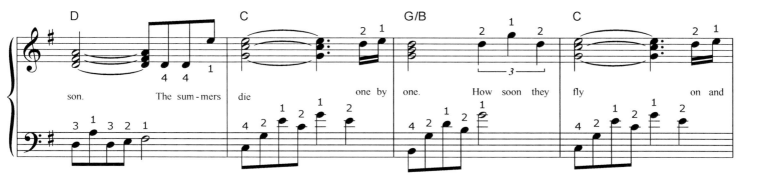

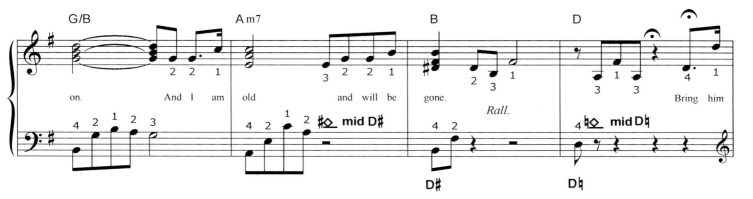

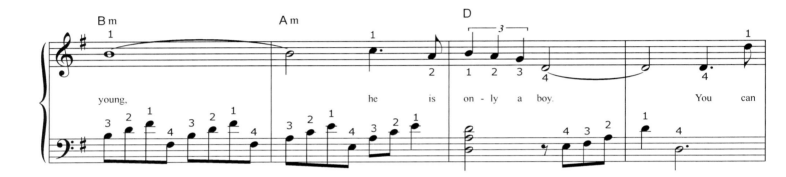

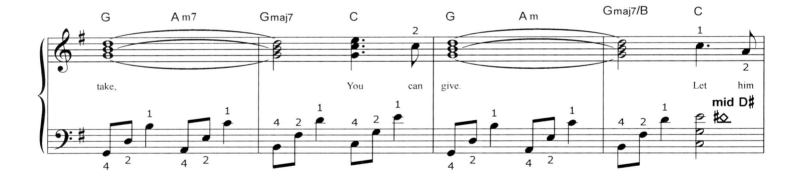

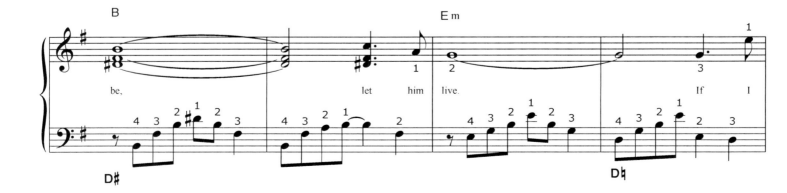

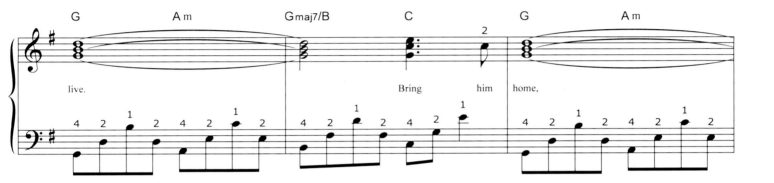

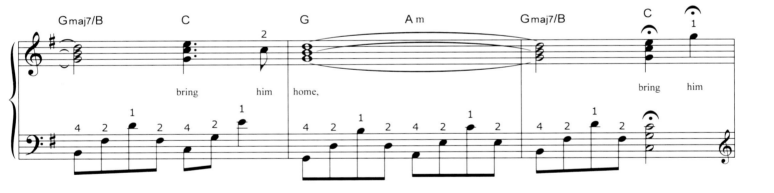

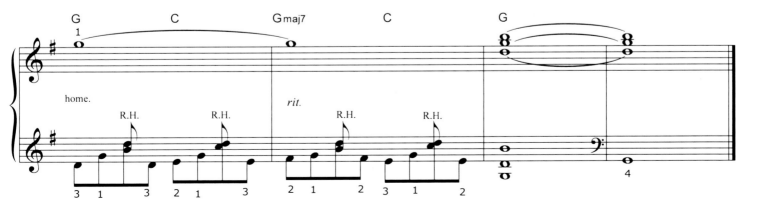

More Harp Arrangements of Pop Music
by Sylvia Woods

Beauty and the Beast

Music from Disney-Pixar's <u>Brave</u>

Castle on a Cloud from <u>Les Misérables</u>

Dead Poets Society

John Denver Love Songs

76 Disney Songs

Fireflies

Music from Disney <u>Frozen</u>

Groovy Songs of the 60s

Four Holiday Favorites

House at Pooh Corner / Return to Pooh Corner

Into the West from <u>The Lord of the Rings</u>

Lennon and McCartney

My Heart Will Go On from <u>Titanic</u>

Over the Rainbow from <u>The Wizard of Oz</u>

22 Romantic Songs

Safe & Sound

Stairway to Heaven

Music from Disney <u>Tangled</u>

Andrew Lloyd Webber Music

The Wizard of Oz

Theme from Disney-Pixar's <u>Up</u>

Available from harp music retailers and www.harpcenter.com

Sylvia Woods Harp Center
P.O. Box 223434, Princeville, HI 96722 U.S.A.

U.S. $7.95

8 88680 01259 5

HL00128726

ISBN 978-0-936661-62-9

9 780936 661629

EXCLUSIVELY DISTRIBUTED BY

HAL•LEONARD®
CORPORATION
7777 W. BLUEMOUND RD. P.O. BOX 13819
MILWAUKEE, WISCONSIN 53213

With many thanks to Paul Baker

© 2014 by Sylvia Woods
Published by Woods Music & Books
P.O. Box 223434, Princeville, HI 96722, U.S.A.
www.harpcenter.com